50 Medieval Banquets and Feasts Recipes

By: Kelly Johnson

Table of Contents

- Roast Suckling Pig
- Pottage with Barley and Vegetables
- Spiced Meat Pie
- Honey-Glazed Roast Chicken
- Almond Milk Porridge
- Baked Trout with Herbs
- Stewed Venison with Red Wine
- Rye Bread with Honey Butter
- Black Pudding Sausages
- Gingered Pork Stew
- Pheasant in a Rich Sauce
- Spiced Wine (Hippocras)
- Mead-Braised Lamb Shanks
- Thick Leek and Onion Soup
- Almond and Raisin Rice
- Barley and Mushroom Casserole
- Sweet and Savory Fruit Tart
- Baked Apples with Spices
- Hard Cheese and Nut Platter
- Roasted Duck with Plum Sauce
- Herb-Infused Meatballs
- Honey and Mustard Glazed Ham
- Mulled Ale with Cinnamon
- Boiled Eel with Herbs
- Goose with Chestnut Stuffing
- Sweetened Oat Cakes
- Smoked Fish with Pickled Vegetables
- Fried Parsnips with Nutmeg
- Gooseberry and Almond Tart
- Custard Tart with Clove and Ginger
- Stewed Pears in Red Wine
- Turnip and Leek Mash
- Roast Quail with Sage
- Braised Cabbage with Caraway
- Buttery Hazelnut Pastries

- Hardtack Biscuits with Cheese
- Stewed Rabbit with Prunes
- Thick Pease Pottage
- Cinnamon and Honey Rice Pudding
- Ale-Braised Beef Ribs
- Roast Boar with Apple Sauce
- Cardamom-Spiced Bread Pudding
- Poached Salmon with Dill
- Roasted Pigeon with Herbs
- Sweetened Almond Soup
- Mashed Chestnuts with Cream
- Elderberry and Honey Compote
- Stuffed Mushrooms with Spices
- Roasted Turnips with Garlic
- Blackberry and Fig Pie

Roast Suckling Pig

Ingredients:

- 1 whole suckling pig (8-12 lbs)
- ¼ cup coarse salt
- 2 tbsp black pepper
- 3 tbsp olive oil or lard
- 2 tbsp honey
- 2 tbsp fresh rosemary, chopped
- 2 tbsp fresh thyme, chopped
- 4 cloves garlic, minced
- 1 apple (for the mouth, optional)

Instructions:

1. Preheat oven to 375°F (190°C).
2. Clean the pig inside and out, pat dry, and rub with salt, pepper, and oil.
3. Mix honey, herbs, and garlic, then rub inside the cavity.
4. Place on a roasting rack in a pan and roast for about 3.5-4 hours, basting occasionally with drippings.
5. Once golden and crispy, remove from oven, let rest, and serve whole with an apple in the mouth for a dramatic presentation.

Pottage with Barley and Vegetables

Ingredients:

- 1 cup barley
- 6 cups vegetable or meat broth
- 2 carrots, diced
- 1 parsnip, diced
- 1 turnip, diced
- 1 leek, chopped
- ½ tsp salt
- ½ tsp ground pepper
- 1 tsp fresh thyme

Instructions:

1. In a large pot, bring broth to a boil.
2. Add barley and simmer for 30 minutes.
3. Add vegetables, salt, pepper, and thyme, and cook for another 20 minutes until vegetables are soft.
4. Serve hot with rye bread.

Spiced Meat Pie

Ingredients:
For the crust:

- 2 ½ cups flour
- ½ cup butter
- ½ tsp salt
- ½ cup warm water

For the filling:

- 1 lb minced pork or beef
- ½ cup currants or raisins
- 1 tsp cinnamon
- ½ tsp cloves
- ½ tsp nutmeg
- ½ tsp black pepper
- 1 tsp salt
- 1 onion, finely chopped
- 1 egg, beaten (for glaze)

Instructions:

1. Preheat oven to 375°F (190°C).
2. Make the crust by mixing flour, butter, salt, and water. Knead and roll out.
3. Mix the filling ingredients in a bowl.
4. Line a pie dish with half the dough, fill with the meat mixture, and cover with the remaining dough.
5. Brush with beaten egg and bake for 40-45 minutes until golden brown.

Honey-Glazed Roast Chicken

Ingredients:

- 1 whole chicken (4-5 lbs)
- 3 tbsp honey
- 2 tbsp butter, melted
- 1 tsp salt
- ½ tsp black pepper
- 1 tsp ground ginger
- ½ tsp cinnamon
- 3 cloves garlic, minced
- 1 cup white wine or ale

Instructions:

1. Preheat oven to 400°F (200°C).
2. Rub the chicken with salt, pepper, ginger, and cinnamon.
3. Mix honey, butter, and garlic, and brush over the chicken.
4. Place in a roasting pan, add wine/ale to the bottom, and roast for about 1 hour 15 minutes, basting every 20 minutes.
5. Let rest before carving.

Almond Milk Porridge

Ingredients:

- 2 cups almond milk
- 1 cup oats or cracked wheat
- 1 tbsp honey
- ½ tsp cinnamon
- ¼ cup chopped almonds

Instructions:

1. Heat almond milk in a saucepan over medium heat.
2. Add oats and stir until thickened (about 10 minutes).
3. Stir in honey and cinnamon, top with almonds, and serve warm.

Baked Trout with Herbs

Ingredients:

- 2 whole trout, cleaned
- 2 tbsp olive oil
- 1 tsp salt
- ½ tsp black pepper
- 2 sprigs rosemary
- 2 sprigs thyme
- 1 lemon, sliced

Instructions:

1. Preheat oven to 375°F (190°C).
2. Rub trout inside and out with olive oil, salt, and pepper.
3. Stuff with herbs and lemon slices.
4. Wrap in parchment or place on a greased baking dish and bake for 20 minutes.

Stewed Venison with Red Wine

Ingredients:

- 2 lbs venison, cubed
- 2 tbsp lard or butter
- 1 onion, chopped
- 2 carrots, diced
- 1 cup red wine
- 2 cups beef broth
- 1 tsp salt
- ½ tsp pepper
- ½ tsp cloves
- 1 bay leaf

Instructions:

1. In a large pot, melt lard and brown venison on all sides.
2. Add onions and carrots, cooking until soft.
3. Pour in wine and broth, add seasonings, and simmer for 2 hours until tender.

Rye Bread with Honey Butter

Ingredients:

For the bread:

- 3 cups rye flour
- 1 ½ cups warm water
- 1 tsp salt
- 1 tsp yeast

For the honey butter:

- ¼ cup butter
- 1 tbsp honey

Instructions:

1. Mix flour, water, salt, and yeast, and knead into a dough. Let rise for 2 hours.
2. Shape into a loaf and bake at 375°F (190°C) for 40 minutes.
3. Mix butter and honey, and spread over warm bread.

Black Pudding Sausages

Ingredients:

- 1 lb pork blood (or substitute with 1 lb minced beef liver)
- ½ lb pork fat, diced
- 1 cup oats
- ½ tsp salt
- ½ tsp black pepper
- ½ tsp thyme
- ½ tsp allspice

Instructions:

1. Mix all ingredients in a bowl.
2. Stuff into sausage casings or shape into patties.
3. Simmer in boiling water for 15 minutes, then fry until crisp.

Gingered Pork Stew

Ingredients:

- 1 lb pork shoulder, cubed
- 2 tbsp lard or butter
- 1 onion, chopped
- 1 tsp ground ginger
- ½ tsp cinnamon
- ½ tsp salt
- ½ tsp black pepper
- 2 cups broth
- 1 apple, diced

Instructions:

1. Brown pork in lard in a large pot.
2. Add onion and spices, cooking until fragrant.
3. Pour in broth and simmer for 1.5 hours.
4. Add diced apple in the last 20 minutes.

Pheasant in a Rich Sauce

Ingredients:

- 1 whole pheasant, cleaned and trussed
- 2 tbsp butter or lard
- 1 onion, chopped
- 1 cup red wine
- 1 cup beef or game broth
- ½ tsp ground cinnamon
- ½ tsp ground cloves
- 1 tbsp honey
- ¼ cup currants or raisins
- ½ tsp black pepper
- Salt to taste

Instructions:

1. Preheat oven to 375°F (190°C).
2. Melt butter in a pan and brown the pheasant on all sides.
3. Transfer to a baking dish. In the same pan, sauté onions until golden.
4. Add wine, broth, spices, honey, and currants, then simmer for 5 minutes.
5. Pour over the pheasant, cover, and roast for 1 hour, basting occasionally.
6. Serve with rustic bread or grains.

Spiced Wine (Hippocras)

Ingredients:

- 1 bottle red wine (750ml)
- ½ cup honey
- 1 tsp ground cinnamon
- ½ tsp ground ginger
- ¼ tsp ground cloves
- ¼ tsp ground nutmeg
- 3 black peppercorns
- 1 orange peel

Instructions:

1. Heat the wine gently in a pot, but do not boil.
2. Stir in honey and spices, then simmer for 5 minutes.
3. Strain through a cloth or fine sieve.
4. Serve warm or cooled.

Mead-Braised Lamb Shanks

Ingredients:

- 2 lamb shanks
- 2 tbsp butter or lard
- 1 onion, chopped
- 2 cloves garlic, minced
- 1 cup mead
- 2 cups beef or lamb broth
- 1 tsp salt
- ½ tsp black pepper
- 1 tsp rosemary
- 1 bay leaf

Instructions:

1. Preheat oven to 325°F (160°C).
2. Brown lamb shanks in butter in a Dutch oven.
3. Add onion and garlic, cooking until fragrant.
4. Pour in mead and broth, add seasonings, and bring to a simmer.
5. Cover and braise in the oven for 2.5 hours.
6. Serve with barley or root vegetables.

Thick Leek and Onion Soup

Ingredients:

- 3 leeks, sliced
- 2 onions, chopped
- 3 tbsp butter
- 4 cups vegetable or chicken broth
- ½ tsp salt
- ½ tsp black pepper
- 1 tsp thyme

Instructions:

1. Melt butter in a pot, then sauté leeks and onions until soft.
2. Add broth, salt, pepper, and thyme, then simmer for 30 minutes.
3. Blend slightly for a thicker texture, or serve as-is.

Almond and Raisin Rice

Ingredients:

- 1 cup long-grain rice
- 2 cups water
- ½ tsp salt
- ¼ cup raisins
- ¼ cup chopped almonds
- ½ tsp cinnamon
- 1 tbsp honey

Instructions:

1. Bring water and salt to a boil, then add rice and simmer until tender.
2. Stir in raisins, almonds, cinnamon, and honey.
3. Let sit for 5 minutes before serving.

Barley and Mushroom Casserole

Ingredients:

- 1 cup pearl barley
- 2 cups vegetable or beef broth
- ½ cup mushrooms, sliced
- 1 onion, chopped
- 2 tbsp butter
- ½ tsp salt
- ½ tsp thyme

Instructions:

1. Preheat oven to 350°F (175°C).
2. Sauté mushrooms and onion in butter.
3. Combine all ingredients in a baking dish.
4. Cover and bake for 45 minutes until barley is tender.

Sweet and Savory Fruit Tart

Ingredients:
For the crust:

- 2 cups flour
- ½ cup butter
- 1 egg yolk
- 2 tbsp honey

For the filling:

- 1 apple, thinly sliced
- ½ cup figs, chopped
- ¼ cup dates, chopped
- ¼ tsp cinnamon
- ¼ tsp nutmeg
- 2 tbsp honey

Instructions:

1. Mix crust ingredients, roll out, and line a tart pan.
2. Arrange fruit on the crust, drizzle with honey, and sprinkle spices.
3. Bake at 375°F (190°C) for 25-30 minutes.

Baked Apples with Spices

Ingredients:

- 4 apples, cored
- ¼ cup honey
- ½ tsp cinnamon
- ¼ tsp nutmeg
- ¼ cup chopped walnuts or almonds

Instructions:

1. Preheat oven to 375°F (190°C).
2. Mix honey, spices, and nuts, then stuff apples.
3. Place in a baking dish with ½ cup water and bake for 30 minutes.

Hard Cheese and Nut Platter

Ingredients:

- 1 wedge aged cheese (like cheddar or gouda)
- ¼ cup almonds
- ¼ cup walnuts
- ¼ cup dried figs
- ¼ cup honey

Instructions:

1. Arrange cheese, nuts, and figs on a wooden board.
2. Drizzle with honey before serving.

Roasted Duck with Plum Sauce

Ingredients:

- 1 whole duck
- 1 tsp salt
- ½ tsp black pepper
- 1 tsp thyme
- 1 cup plums, chopped
- ¼ cup honey
- ¼ cup red wine
- ½ tsp cinnamon

Instructions:

1. Preheat oven to 375°F (190°C).
2. Season duck with salt, pepper, and thyme, then roast for 1.5-2 hours.
3. Simmer plums, honey, wine, and cinnamon in a pot until thickened.
4. Serve sauce over carved duck.

Herb-Infused Meatballs

Ingredients:

- 1 lb ground beef or lamb
- ½ cup breadcrumbs
- 1 egg
- 1 tsp salt
- ½ tsp black pepper
- ½ tsp thyme
- ½ tsp rosemary
- ½ tsp sage
- 2 cloves garlic, minced
- 2 tbsp butter

Instructions:

1. Mix all ingredients except butter in a bowl.
2. Form small meatballs and chill for 15 minutes.
3. Heat butter in a pan and fry meatballs until browned on all sides.
4. Serve with rustic bread or a spiced sauce.

Honey and Mustard Glazed Ham

Ingredients:

- 1 cured ham (about 5 lbs)
- ½ cup honey
- ¼ cup whole grain mustard
- 1 tsp ground cloves
- 1 tsp black pepper

Instructions:

1. Preheat oven to 350°F (175°C).
2. Score the ham and place it in a roasting pan.
3. Mix honey, mustard, cloves, and pepper, then brush over the ham.
4. Roast for 1.5 hours, basting every 30 minutes.
5. Let rest before slicing.

Mulled Ale with Cinnamon

Ingredients:

- 1 quart dark ale
- 2 tbsp honey
- 1 cinnamon stick
- 3 cloves
- 1 slice fresh ginger
- 1 orange peel

Instructions:

1. Heat ale in a pot, but do not boil.
2. Stir in honey and add spices and orange peel.
3. Simmer for 10 minutes, then strain before serving warm.

Boiled Eel with Herbs

Ingredients:

- 2 fresh eels, cleaned and cut into pieces
- 4 cups water
- 1 tsp salt
- ½ tsp black pepper
- 1 bay leaf
- 1 sprig thyme
- ½ cup white wine
- 1 onion, chopped

Instructions:

1. Bring water, wine, onion, salt, and herbs to a boil.
2. Add eel pieces and simmer for 20-25 minutes.
3. Remove eel and serve with rustic bread and mustard.

Goose with Chestnut Stuffing

Ingredients:

- 1 whole goose
- 1 tsp salt
- ½ tsp black pepper
- 1 tsp thyme
- 1 cup chestnuts, roasted and chopped
- 1 onion, diced
- 1 apple, chopped
- ½ cup breadcrumbs
- ¼ cup butter, melted

Instructions:

1. Preheat oven to 375°F (190°C).
2. Mix chestnuts, onion, apple, breadcrumbs, and butter for the stuffing.
3. Stuff the goose, then season with salt, pepper, and thyme.
4. Roast for 2.5 hours, basting occasionally.
5. Let rest before carving.

Sweetened Oat Cakes

Ingredients:

- 2 cups oats
- ½ cup honey
- ¼ cup butter, melted
- ½ tsp cinnamon
- ¼ cup chopped nuts (optional)

Instructions:

1. Preheat oven to 350°F (175°C).
2. Mix all ingredients and press into a baking dish.
3. Bake for 15-20 minutes until golden brown.
4. Let cool before cutting into squares.

Smoked Fish with Pickled Vegetables

Ingredients:

- 1 lb smoked fish (trout, herring, or mackerel)
- 1 cup vinegar
- ½ cup water
- 1 tsp salt
- ½ tsp sugar
- 1 bay leaf
- ½ tsp mustard seeds
- 1 carrot, thinly sliced
- 1 onion, thinly sliced

Instructions:

1. Heat vinegar, water, salt, sugar, and spices in a pot.
2. Pour over sliced carrots and onions, then let cool.
3. Serve pickled vegetables with smoked fish.

Fried Parsnips with Nutmeg

Ingredients:

- 3 parsnips, peeled and sliced
- 2 tbsp butter
- ½ tsp salt
- ¼ tsp nutmeg

Instructions:

1. Boil parsnips for 5 minutes, then drain.
2. Heat butter in a pan and fry parsnips until golden brown.
3. Sprinkle with salt and nutmeg before serving.

Gooseberry and Almond Tart

Ingredients:

For the crust:

- 2 cups flour
- ½ cup butter
- 1 egg yolk
- 2 tbsp honey

For the filling:

- 1 cup gooseberries
- ½ cup almonds, chopped
- ¼ cup honey
- ½ tsp cinnamon

Instructions:

1. Preheat oven to 375°F (190°C).
2. Mix crust ingredients, roll out, and line a tart pan.
3. Arrange gooseberries and almonds on top, then drizzle with honey and cinnamon.
4. Bake for 25-30 minutes until golden brown.

Custard Tart with Clove and Ginger

Ingredients:

- 1 pre-made pie crust (or homemade shortcrust pastry)
- 2 cups milk
- 3 egg yolks
- ¼ cup honey
- ½ tsp ground ginger
- ¼ tsp ground cloves
- ½ tsp cinnamon
- 1 tsp vanilla extract

Instructions:

1. Preheat oven to 350°F (175°C).
2. Roll out the pie crust and place it into a tart pan. Pre-bake for 10 minutes.
3. In a saucepan, heat milk with honey, ginger, cloves, cinnamon, and vanilla (do not boil).
4. Whisk egg yolks in a bowl, then slowly add the warm milk mixture while whisking.
5. Pour the mixture into the pre-baked tart shell.
6. Bake for 25-30 minutes or until the custard is set. Let cool before serving.

Stewed Pears in Red Wine

Ingredients:

- 4 firm pears, peeled and halved
- 2 cups red wine
- ½ cup honey
- 1 cinnamon stick
- 3 cloves
- 1 orange peel

Instructions:

1. In a pot, combine wine, honey, cinnamon, cloves, and orange peel. Bring to a simmer.
2. Add pears and simmer for 20-25 minutes until tender.
3. Remove pears and reduce the sauce until syrupy.
4. Serve pears with the sauce drizzled on top.

Turnip and Leek Mash

Ingredients:

- 3 turnips, peeled and diced
- 2 leeks, sliced
- 2 tbsp butter
- ½ tsp salt
- ½ tsp black pepper

Instructions:

1. Boil turnips until soft (about 15 minutes), then drain.
2. Sauté leeks in butter until softened.
3. Mash turnips with leeks, salt, and pepper until smooth.

Roast Quail with Sage

Ingredients:

- 4 whole quails
- 2 tbsp olive oil or butter
- 1 tsp salt
- ½ tsp black pepper
- 1 tsp sage, chopped
- 2 cloves garlic, minced

Instructions:

1. Preheat oven to 400°F (200°C).
2. Rub quails with olive oil, salt, pepper, garlic, and sage.
3. Roast for 20-25 minutes until golden brown.

Braised Cabbage with Caraway

Ingredients:

- 1 small cabbage, shredded
- 1 tbsp butter
- 1 tsp caraway seeds
- ½ tsp salt
- ¼ cup vinegar

Instructions:

1. Melt butter in a pan, add cabbage and sauté for 5 minutes.
2. Add caraway seeds, salt, and vinegar.
3. Simmer for 10-15 minutes until tender.

Buttery Hazelnut Pastries

Ingredients:

- 1 cup flour
- ½ cup butter, softened
- ¼ cup honey
- ½ cup ground hazelnuts

Instructions:

1. Preheat oven to 350°F (175°C).
2. Mix all ingredients into a dough. Roll out and cut into small shapes.
3. Bake for 15-18 minutes until golden.

Hardtack Biscuits with Cheese

Ingredients:

- 2 cups flour
- 1 tsp salt
- ¾ cup water
- ½ cup hard cheese, grated

Instructions:

1. Preheat oven to 375°F (190°C).
2. Mix all ingredients into a stiff dough. Roll out and cut into squares.
3. Bake for 30-40 minutes until dry and hard.

Stewed Rabbit with Prunes

Ingredients:

- 1 rabbit, cut into pieces
- 2 tbsp butter
- 1 onion, chopped
- 1 cup red wine
- 1 cup beef broth
- ½ tsp salt
- ½ tsp black pepper
- ½ cup prunes

Instructions:

1. Brown rabbit pieces in butter, then remove.
2. Sauté onion, then deglaze with wine and broth.
3. Return rabbit to the pot, add salt, pepper, and prunes.
4. Simmer for 1.5 hours until tender.

Thick Pease Pottage

Ingredients:

- 1 cup dried split peas
- 4 cups water
- 1 onion, chopped
- 1 carrot, diced
- 1 tsp salt
- ½ tsp black pepper

Instructions:

1. Boil peas in water until soft (about 1 hour).
2. Add onion, carrot, salt, and pepper, then simmer for 30 minutes.

Cinnamon and Honey Rice Pudding

Ingredients:

- 1 cup rice
- 2 cups milk
- ¼ cup honey
- 1 tsp cinnamon

Instructions:

1. Cook rice in milk until soft.
2. Stir in honey and cinnamon. Serve warm.

Ale-Braised Beef Ribs

Ingredients:

- 2 lbs beef short ribs
- 1 tbsp olive oil
- 1 onion, chopped
- 2 cloves garlic, minced
- 2 cups dark ale
- 1 cup beef broth
- 1 tbsp honey
- 1 tsp black pepper
- 1 tsp salt
- 1 bay leaf

Instructions:

1. In a heavy pot or Dutch oven, heat olive oil over medium-high heat. Brown the ribs on all sides; remove and set aside.
2. Sauté the chopped onion and garlic until softened.
3. Add the ale and beef broth, stirring in honey, salt, pepper, and bay leaf.
4. Return the ribs to the pot, bring the liquid to a simmer, then cover and cook on low heat for about 2 hours until the meat is tender.
5. Serve hot with rustic bread or over mashed vegetables.

Roast Boar with Apple Sauce

Ingredients:

- 3 lbs pork shoulder
- 2 tbsp olive oil
- 1 tsp salt
- 1 tsp black pepper
- 2 tsp rosemary
- 2 apples, peeled and chopped
- ½ cup apple cider
- 1 tbsp honey
- ½ tsp cinnamon

Instructions:

1. Preheat your oven to 375°F (190°C).
2. Rub the pork shoulder with olive oil, salt, pepper, and rosemary.
3. Place in a roasting pan and roast for about 2 hours until tender.
4. Meanwhile, in a saucepan, combine the apples, apple cider, honey, and cinnamon. Simmer until the apples are soft, then mash or blend into a sauce.
5. Serve the roast pork with a generous helping of apple sauce.

Cardamom-Spiced Bread Pudding

Ingredients:

- 4 cups stale bread, cubed
- 2 cups milk
- 2 eggs
- ¼ cup honey
- 1 tsp ground cardamom
- ½ tsp ground cinnamon
- ¼ cup raisins (optional)

Instructions:

1. Preheat oven to 350°F (175°C).
2. In a large bowl, soak the bread cubes in milk for 10 minutes.
3. Whisk together eggs, honey, cardamom, and cinnamon; mix into the soaked bread along with raisins if using.
4. Transfer the mixture into a greased baking dish and bake for 35 minutes until set and golden.

Poached Salmon with Dill

Ingredients:

- 2 salmon fillets
- 2 cups water
- ½ cup white wine
- 1 lemon, thinly sliced
- 2 tsp fresh dill, chopped
- ½ tsp salt

Instructions:

1. In a large pot, combine water, white wine, lemon slices, and salt. Bring to a gentle simmer.
2. Add the salmon fillets and poach for about 10 minutes or until just cooked through.
3. Sprinkle with fresh dill and serve immediately.

Roasted Pigeon with Herbs

Ingredients:

- 2 whole pigeons (or 2 Cornish game hens)
- 2 tbsp butter
- 1 tsp salt
- ½ tsp black pepper
- 1 tsp thyme
- 1 tsp rosemary

Instructions:

1. Preheat the oven to 375°F (190°C).
2. Rub the birds with melted butter and season inside and out with salt, pepper, thyme, and rosemary.
3. Roast for 40–45 minutes, basting occasionally.
4. Let rest for a few minutes before serving.

Sweetened Almond Soup

Ingredients:

- 1 cup ground almonds
- 2 cups milk (or almond milk for extra nuttiness)
- ¼ cup honey
- ½ tsp ground cinnamon

Instructions:

1. In a saucepan, combine milk and ground almonds.
2. Heat gently while stirring, then add honey and cinnamon.
3. Allow to simmer for about 10 minutes, stirring occasionally.
4. Serve warm.

Mashed Chestnuts with Cream

Ingredients:

- 1 lb chestnuts, roasted and peeled
- 1 cup heavy cream
- 2 tbsp butter
- 1 tsp salt

Instructions:

1. Boil or steam chestnuts until very soft (about 20 minutes).
2. Mash chestnuts in a bowl, then stir in warm heavy cream, butter, and salt until smooth and creamy.
3. Serve as a side dish.

Elderberry and Honey Compote

Ingredients:

- 2 cups elderberries (or substitute with blackberries)
- ¼ cup honey
- ½ tsp ground cinnamon

Instructions:

1. In a small saucepan, combine the berries, honey, and cinnamon.
2. Simmer over medium-low heat for about 10 minutes until the mixture thickens slightly.
3. Let cool slightly and serve as a condiment or dessert topping.

Stuffed Mushrooms with Spices

Ingredients:

- 8 large mushrooms, stems removed
- ½ cup breadcrumbs
- 1 tbsp butter
- 1 tsp dried thyme
- ½ tsp black pepper
- 1 small garlic clove, minced

Instructions:

1. Preheat oven to 375°F (190°C).
2. In a bowl, mix breadcrumbs, melted butter, thyme, pepper, and garlic.
3. Stuff each mushroom cap with the breadcrumb mixture.
4. Place on a baking sheet and bake for 15 minutes until the mushrooms are tender and the topping is golden.

Roasted Turnips with Garlic

Ingredients:

- 4 turnips, peeled and cubed
- 2 tbsp olive oil
- 2 cloves garlic, minced
- 1 tsp salt

Instructions:

1. Preheat oven to 400°F (200°C).
2. Toss turnip cubes with olive oil, garlic, and salt.
3. Spread on a baking sheet and roast for 25 minutes or until golden and tender.

Blackberry and Fig Pie

Ingredients:

- 1 pre-made pie crust (or homemade pastry)
- 2 cups blackberries
- 1 cup figs, chopped
- ¼ cup honey
- 1 tsp cinnamon

Instructions:

1. Preheat oven to 375°F (190°C).
2. In a bowl, mix blackberries, chopped figs, honey, and cinnamon.
3. Fill the pie crust with the fruit mixture.
4. Bake for 35 minutes until the crust is golden and the filling is bubbly.
5. Cool before serving.

www.ingramcontent.com/pod-product-compliance
Lightning Source LLC
LaVergne TN
LVHW081342060526
838201LV00055B/2793